Contents

6
7
8
9
10

Introduction

This guide provides good practice advice for dealing with discipline and grievances in the workplace. It complements the *Acas Code of Practice* on disciplinary and grievance procedures. Extracts from the Code of Practice are reproduced in shaded boxes accompanied by further practical advice and guidance.

> **Extract: Acas Code of Practice on disciplinary and grievance procedures**
>
> This Code is designed to help employers, employees and their representatives deal with disciplinary and grievance situations in the workplace.

The Acas Code of Practice sets out principles for handling disciplinary and grievance situations in the workplace. This guide provides more detailed advice and guidance that employers and employees will often find helpful both in general terms and in individual cases.

Employment tribunals are legally required to take the Acas Code of Practice into account when considering relevant cases. Tribunals will also be able to adjust any compensatory awards made in these cases by up to 25 per cent for unreasonable failure to comply with any provision of the Code. This means that if the tribunal feels that an employer has unreasonably failed to follow the guidance set out in the Code they can increase any award they have made by up to 25 per cent. Conversely, if they feel an employee has unreasonably failed to follow the guidance set out in the Code they can reduce any award they have made by up to 25 per cent.

Employment tribunals are not required to have regard to guidance in this booklet that does not form part of the Code.

If you are (or expect to be) affected by such an issue, see Appendix 6 on important changes to making a tribunal claim.

The law on unfair dismissal requires employers to act reasonably when dealing with disciplinary issues. What is classed as reasonable behaviour will depend on the circumstances of each case, and is ultimately a matter for employment tribunals to decide. However, the core principles are set out in the Acas Code of Practice.

The foreword to the Code and this guide emphasise that employers and employees should always seek to resolve disciplinary and grievance issues in the workplace. If discipline and grievance issues are settled at an early stage they are normally less time-consuming and less likely to damage working relationships.

Good employment relations practices – including for recruitment, induction training, communications and consultation – can prevent many discipline and grievance problems arising. Organisations are also more likely to have positive employment relationships if they make efforts to gain their employees' commitment through:

- showing them clear leadership and letting them know how they can contribute

- engaging them in their work and giving them the power to make some decisions themselves rather than trying to control and restrict them

- showing them respect and appreciation

- giving them ways to voice their views and concerns.

Acas provides comprehensive guidance on employment issues which you can download from our website, and information about suitable training. For further details see the Acas website www.acas.org. uk or call the Acas Helpline **0300 123 1100** (Open Monday – Friday 8am–8pm & Saturday 9am–1pm).

Handling discipline – an overview

- Always follow the Acas *Code of Practice on disciplinary and grievance procedures*
- It may be helpful to consider **mediation** at any stage – see p7

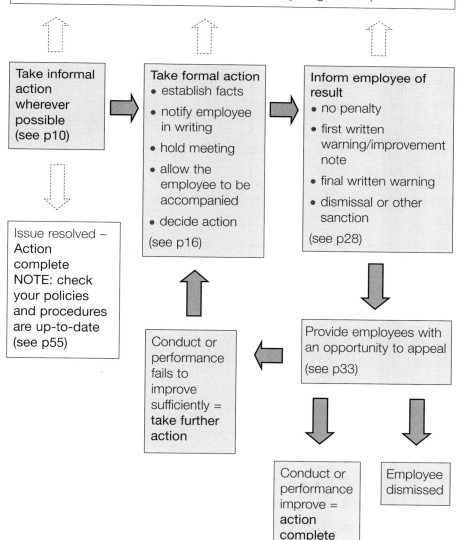

Take informal action wherever possible (see p10)

Take formal action
- establish facts
- notify employee in writing
- hold meeting
- allow the employee to be accompanied
- decide action

(see p16)

Inform employee of result
- no penalty
- first written warning/improvement note
- final written warning
- dismissal or other sanction

(see p28)

Issue resolved – **Action complete** NOTE: check your policies and procedures are up-to-date (see p55)

Conduct or performance fails to improve sufficiently = **take further action**

Provide employees with an opportunity to appeal (see p33)

Conduct or performance improve = **action complete**

Employee dismissed

Handling grievances – an overview

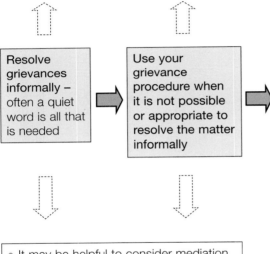

Always follow the Acas *Code of Practice on disciplinary and grievance procedures*

Resolve grievances informally – often a quiet word is all that is needed

Use your grievance procedure when it is not possible or appropriate to resolve the matter informally

- Employee to let the employer know the grievance in writing
- Meeting to discuss the grievance
- Allow the employee to be accompanied at the meeting
- Decide on appropriate action
- Allow the employee to appeal if not satisfied

(see p45-51)

- It may be helpful to consider mediation at any stage of a dispute. For more information (see p7)
- Train managers and employee representatives to handle grievances effectively

Deal with appeal impartially and where possible by a manager not previously involved

Using mediation

An independent third party or mediator can sometimes help resolve disciplinary or grievance issues. Mediation is a voluntary process where the mediator helps two or more people in dispute to attempt to reach an agreement. Any agreement comes from those in dispute, not from the mediator. The mediator is not there to judge, to say one person is right and the other wrong, or to tell those involved in the mediation what they should do. The mediator is in charge of the process of seeking to resolve the problem but not the outcome.

Mediators may be employees trained and accredited by an external mediation service who act as internal mediators in addition to their day jobs. Or they may be from an external mediation provider. They can work individually or in pairs as co-mediators.

There are no hard-and-fast rules for when mediation is appropriate but it can be used:

- for conflict involving colleagues of a similar job or grade, or between a line manager and their staff

- at any stage in the conflict as long as any ongoing formal procedures are put in abeyance, or where mediation is included as a stage in the procedures themselves

- to rebuild relationships after a formal dispute has been resolved

- to address a range of issues, including relationship breakdown, personality clashes, communication problems, bullying and harassment.

In some organisations mediation is written into formal discipline and grievance procedures as an optional stage. Where this is not the case, it is useful to be clear about whether the discipline and grievance procedure can be suspended if mediation is deemed to be an appropriate method of resolving the dispute.

Grievances most obviously lend themselves to the possibility of mediation. Managers may not always see it as appropriate to surrender their discretion in relation to disciplinary issues where they believe a point of principle is at stake, such as misconduct or poor performance. However, disciplinary and grievance issues can become blurred, and the employer may prefer to tackle the underlying relationship issues by means of mediation.

Cases unsuitable for mediation

Mediation may not be suitable if:

● used as a first resort – because people should be encouraged to speak to each other and talk to their manager before they seek a solution via mediation

● it is used by a manager to avoid their managerial responsibilities

● a decision about right or wrong is needed, for example where there is possible criminal activity

● the individual bringing a discrimination or harassment case wants it investigated

● the parties do not have the power to settle the issue

● one side is completely intransigent and using mediation will only raise unrealistic expectations of a positive outcome.

For more information about mediation see the Acas website at www.acas.org.uk and the Acas/CIPD guide *Mediation: An employer's guide* which can be downloaded from the website.

Discipline
Keys to handling disciplinary problems in the workplace

Discipline

Keys to handling disciplinary problems in the workplace

Resolve discipline issues informally

Cases of minor misconduct or unsatisfactory performance are usually best dealt with informally. A quiet word is often all that is required to improve an employee's conduct or performance. In some cases additional training, coaching and advice may be what is needed. An informal approach may be particularly helpful in small firms, where problems can be resolved quickly and confidentially. There will be situations where matters are more serious or where an informal approach has been tried but is not working.

If informal action does not bring about an improvement, or the misconduct or unsatisfactory performance is considered too serious to be classed as minor, employers should provide employees with a clear signal of their dissatisfaction by taking formal action.

> ### Discipline in practice 1
> A valued and generally reliable employee is late for work on a number of occasions causing difficulty for other staff who have to provide cover.
>
> You talk to the employee on his own and he reveals that he has recently split up with his wife and he now has to take the children to school on the way to work. You agree a temporary adjustment to his start and finish times and he undertakes to make arrangements for 'school run' cover which solves the problem. You decide that formal disciplinary action is not appropriate.

How should it be done?
Talk to the employee in private. This should be a two-way discussion, aimed at discussing possible shortcomings in conduct or performance and encouraging improvement. Criticism should be constructive, with the emphasis being on finding ways for the employee to improve and for the improvement to be sustained.

Listen to whatever the employee has to say about the issue. It may become evident there is no problem – if so make this clear to the employee.

Where improvement is required make sure the employee understands what needs to be done, how their performance or conduct will be reviewed, and over what period. It may be useful to confirm in writing what has been decided.

Be careful that any informal action does not turn into formal disciplinary action, as this may unintentionally deny the employee certain rights, such as the right to be accompanied (see p23). If, during the discussion, it becomes obvious that the matter may be more serious, the meeting should be adjourned. The employee should be told that the matter will be continued under the formal disciplinary procedure.

Keep brief notes of any agreed informal action for reference purposes. There should be reviews of progress over specified periods.

Consider at any stage whether the use of an independent mediator may be helpful (see p7).

Develop rules and procedures

Extract: Acas Code of Practice on disciplinary and grievance procedures

Fairness and transparency are promoted by developing and using rules and procedures for handling disciplinary and grievance situations. These should be set down in writing, be specific and clear. Employees and, where appropriate, their representatives should be involved in the development of rules and procedures. It is also important to help employees and managers understand what the rules and procedures are, where they can be found and how they are to be used.

Rules and performance standards

Clear rules benefit employees and set standards of conduct. They also help employers to act fairly and consistently.

Employers should also set standards of performance so that employees know what is expected of them. This is usually done as part of an organisation's performance management which will involve agreeing objectives and reviewing performance on a regular basis.

What should rules cover?

Different organisations will have different requirements but rules often cover such matters as:

- timekeeping

- absence[1]

- health and safety

- use of organisation facilities

- discrimination, bullying and harassment

- personal appearance

- the types of conduct that might be considered as 'gross misconduct' (see p31).

How should rules be drawn up and communicated?

Rules are likely to be more effective if they are accepted as reasonable by those covered by them and those who operate them. It is good practice to develop rules in consultation with employees (and their representatives where appropriate) and those who will have responsibility for applying them.

Unless there are reasons why different sets of rules apply to different groups they should apply to all employees at all levels in the organisation.

The rules should not discriminate on the grounds of sex, transgender, marital or civil partnership status, racial group, sexual orientation, religion or belief, disability[2] or age[3].

Writing down the rules helps both managers and employees to know what is expected of them. The rules should be made clear to employees. Ideally employees should be given their own printed copy of the rules or written information about how to access them – eg on the organisation's Intranet or in their handbook. Employees are entitled to a written statement of employment particulars which must include a note about disciplinary rules and procedures[4].

In a small organisation, it may be sufficient for rules to be displayed in a prominent place. See Appendix 1 for a checklist 'Disciplinary rules for small organisations'.

Special attention should be paid to ensure that rules are understood by any employees without recent experience of working life (for instance young people or those returning to work after a lengthy break), and by employees whose English or reading ability is limited or who have a disability such as visual impairment.

Why have a disciplinary procedure?

A disciplinary procedure is the means by which rules are observed and standards are maintained. The procedure should be used primarily to help and encourage employees to improve rather than just as a way of imposing punishment. It provides a method of dealing with any apparent shortcomings in conduct or performance and can help an employee to become effective again. The procedure should be fair, effective, and consistently applied.

Extract: Acas Code of Practice on disciplinary and grievance procedures

Disciplinary situations include misconduct and/or poor performance. If employers have a separate capability procedure they may prefer to address performance issues under this procedure. If so, however, the basic principles of fairness set out in this Code should still be followed, albeit that they may need to be adapted.

What should disciplinary procedures contain?

When drawing up and applying procedures, employers should always bear in mind principles of fairness. For example, employees should be informed of the allegations against them, together with the supporting evidence, in advance of the meeting. Employees should be given the opportunity to challenge the allegations before decisions are reached and should be provided with a right to appeal. Good disciplinary procedures should:

- be in writing

- be non-discriminatory

- provide for matters to be dealt with speedily

- allow for information to be kept confidential

- tell employees what disciplinary action might be taken

- say what levels of management have the authority to take the various forms of disciplinary action

- require employees to be informed of the complaints against them and supporting evidence, before a disciplinary meeting

- give employees a chance to have their say before management reaches a decision

- provide employees with the right to be accompanied

- provide that no employee is dismissed for a first breach of discipline, except in cases of gross misconduct

2

- require management to investigate fully before any disciplinary action is taken

- ensure that employees are given an explanation for any sanction and allow employees to appeal against a decision

- apply to all employees, irrespective of their length of service, status or say if there are different rules for different groups and ensure that:

  - any investigatory period of suspension is with pay, and specify how pay is to be calculated during this period. If, exceptionally, suspension is to be without pay, this must be provided for in the contract of employment

  - any suspension is brief, and is never used as a sanction against the employee prior to a disciplinary meeting and decision. Keep the employee informed of progress

  - the employee will be heard in good faith and that there is no pre-judgement of the issue

  - where the facts are in dispute, no disciplinary penalty is imposed until the case has been carefully investigated, and there is a reasonably held belief that the employee committed the act in question.

Samples of disciplinary procedures are at Appendix 2 – Sample disciplinary and grievance procedures, and may be adapted according to the requirements of the organisation.

Reviewing rules and procedures

Keep rules and procedures under review to make sure they are always relevant and effective. Address any shortcomings as they arise. Employees and their representatives should be consulted before new or additional rules are introduced.

Training

Good training helps managers achieve positive outcomes, reducing the need for any further disciplinary action. Those responsible for using and operating the disciplinary rules and procedures, including managers at all levels, should be trained for the task. Ignoring or circumventing the procedures when dismissing an employee is likely to have a bearing on the outcome of any subsequent employment tribunal claim. If the organisation recognises trade unions, or there is any other form of employee representation, it can be useful to undertake training on a joint basis – everyone then has the same understanding and has an opportunity to work through the procedure, clarifying any issues that might arise. For information about suitable training see the Acas website www.acas.org.uk/training.

Keeping written records

What records should be kept?

The foreword to the Code of Practice advises employers to keep a written record of any disciplinary or grievances cases they deal with.

Records should include:

- the complaint against the employee

- the employee's defence

- findings made and actions taken

- the reason for actions taken

- whether an appeal was lodged

- the outcome of the appeal

- any grievances raised during the disciplinary procedure

- subsequent developments

- notes of any formal meetings.

Records should be treated as confidential and be kept no longer than necessary in accordance with the Data Protection Act 1998. This Act gives individuals the right to request and have access to certain personal data. The Information Commissioner has produced Codes of Practice covering recruitment and selection, employment records, monitoring at work and information about an employee's health5. The data protection principles are outlined at Appendix 5.

Copies of meeting records should be given to the employee including copies of any formal minutes that may have been taken. In certain circumstances (for example to protect a witness) the employer might withhold some information.

2

Dealing fairly with formal disciplinary action

Extract: Acas Code of Practice on disciplinary and grievance procedures*

Where some form of formal action is needed, what action is reasonable or justified will depend on all the circumstances of the particular case. Employment tribunals will take the size and resources of an employer into account when deciding on relevant cases and it may sometimes not be practicable for all employers to take all of the steps set out in this Code.

That said, whenever a disciplinary or grievance process is being followed it is important to deal with issues fairly. There are a number of elements to this:

- Employers and employees should raise and deal with issues promptly and should not unreasonably delay meetings, decisions or confirmation of those decisions.

- Employers and employees should act consistently.

- Employers should carry out any necessary investigations, to establish the facts of the case.

- Employers should inform employees of the basis of the problem and give them an opportunity to put their case in response before any decisions are made.

- Employers should allow employees to be accompanied at any formal disciplinary or grievance meeting.

- Employers should allow an employee to appeal against any formal decision made.

*Refer to Appendix 6 which outlines important changes to making Employment tribunal claims.

The following pages give detailed guidance on handling formal disciplinary issues. Always bear in mind the need for fairness when following procedures taking account of the elements from the Acas Code of Practice reproduced above. Dealing with absence is only one of any number of issues where disciplinary action may be considered. It can, however, raise particular problems and is dealt with separately at Appendix 4 – Dealing with absence.

Establishing the facts

Investigating cases

When investigating a disciplinary matter take care to deal with the employee in a fair and reasonable manner. The nature and extent of the investigations will depend on the seriousness of the matter and the more serious it is then the more thorough the investigation should be. It is important to keep an open mind and look for evidence which supports the employee's case as well as evidence against.

It is not always necessary to hold an investigatory meeting (often called a fact finding meeting). If a meeting is held, give the employee advance warning and time to prepare.

Any investigatory meeting should be conducted by a management representative and should be confined to establishing the facts of the case. It is important that disciplinary action is not considered at an investigatory meeting. If it becomes apparent that formal disciplinary action may be needed then this should be dealt with at a formal meeting at which the employee will have the statutory right to be accompanied. See also 'Use of external consultants' on p37.

Suspension

There may be instances where suspension with pay is necessary while investigations are carried out. For example where relationships have broken down, in gross misconduct cases or where there are risks to an employee's or the company's property or responsibilities to other parties. Exceptionally you may wish to consider suspension with pay where you have reasonable grounds for concern that evidence has been tampered with, destroyed or witnesses pressurised before the meeting.

Suspension with pay should only be imposed after careful consideration and should be reviewed to ensure it is not unnecessarily protracted. It should be made clear that suspension is not an assumption of guilt and is not considered a disciplinary sanction.

Informing the employee

Extract: Acas Code of Practice on disciplinary and grievance procedures

If it is decided that there is a disciplinary case to answer, the employee should be notified of this in writing. This notification should contain sufficient information about the alleged misconduct or poor performance and its possible consequences to enable the employee to prepare to answer the case at a disciplinary meeting. It would normally be appropriate to provide copies of any written evidence, which may include any witness statements, with the notification.

The notification should also give details of the time and venue for the disciplinary meeting and advise the employee of their right to be accompanied at the meeting.

As well notifying the nature of the complaint and the right to be accompanied (see p23) the employee should also be told about the procedure to be followed.

A sample letter inviting an employee to a meeting is at Appendix 3.

Holding a disciplinary meeting

Extract: Acas Code of Practice on disciplinary and grievance procedures

The meeting should be held without unreasonable delay whilst allowing the employee reasonable time to prepare their case.

Employers and employees (and their companions) should make every effort to attend the meeting. At the meeting the employer should explain the complaint against the employee and go through the evidence that has been gathered. The employee should be allowed to set out their case and answer any allegations that have been made. The employee should also be given a reasonable opportunity to ask questions, present evidence and call relevant witnesses. They should also be given an opportunity to raise points about any information provided by witnesses. Where an employer or employee intends to call relevant witnesses they should give advance notice that they intend to do this.

Preparing for the meeting

You should:

- ensure that all the relevant facts are available, such as disciplinary records and any other relevant documents (for instance absence or sickness records) and, where appropriate, written statements from witnesses

- where possible arrange for someone who is not involved in the case to take a note of the meeting and to act as a witness to what was said

- check if there are any special circumstances to be taken into account. For example, are there personal or other outside issues affecting performance or conduct?

- be careful when dealing with evidence from a person who wishes to remain anonymous. Take written statements, seek corroborative evidence and check that the person's motives are genuine[6]

- consider what explanations may be offered by the employee, and if possible check them out beforehand

- allow the employee time to prepare his or her case. Copies of any relevant papers and witness statements should be made available to the employee in advance

- if the employee concerned is a trade union representative discuss the case with a trade union full-time official after obtaining the employee's agreement. This is because the action may be seen as an attack on the union

- arrange a time for the meeting, which should be held as privately as possible, in a suitable room, and where there will be no interruptions. The employee may offer a reasonable alternative time within five days of the original date if their chosen companion cannot attend. You may also arrange another meeting if an employee fails to attend through circumstances outside their control, such as illness

- try and get a written statement from any witness from outside the organisation who is not prepared to or is unable to attend the meeting

- allow the employee to call witnesses or submit witness statements

- consider the provision of an interpreter or facilitator if there are understanding or language difficulties (perhaps a friend of the employee, or a co-employee). This person may need to attend in addition to the companion though ideally one person should carry out both roles

- make provision for any reasonable adjustments to accommodate the needs of a person with disabilities

- think about the structure of the meeting and make a list of points you will wish to cover.

What if an employee repeatedly fails to attend a meeting?

There may be occasions when an employee is repeatedly unable or unwilling to attend a meeting. This may be for various reasons, including genuine illness or a refusal to face up to the issue. Employers will need to consider all the facts and come to a reasonable decision on how to proceed. Considerations may include:

- any rules the organisation has for dealing with failure to attend disciplinary meetings

- the seriousness of the disciplinary issue under consideration

- the employee's disciplinary record (including current warnings), general work record, work experience, position and length of service

- medical opinion on whether the employee is fit to attend the meeting

- how similar cases in the past have been dealt with.

Where an employee continues to be unavailable to attend a meeting the employer may conclude that a decision will be made on the evidence available. The employee should be informed where this is to be the case. See also Appendix 4 'Dealing with absence'.

How should the disciplinary meeting be conducted?

Remember that the point of the meeting is to establish the facts, not catch people out. The meetings may not proceed in neat, orderly stages but it is good practice to:

- introduce those present to the employee and explain why they are there

- introduce and explain the role of the accompanying person if present

- explain that the purpose of the meeting is to consider whether disciplinary action should be taken in accordance with the organisation's disciplinary procedure

- explain how the meeting will be conducted.

Statement of the complaint

State precisely what the complaint is and outline the case briefly by going through the evidence that has been gathered. Ensure that the employee and his or her representative or accompanying person are allowed to see any statements made by witnesses and question them.

Employee's reply

Give the employee the opportunity to state their case and answer any allegations that have been made. They should be able to ask questions, present evidence and call witnesses. The accompanying person may also ask questions and should be able to confer privately with the employee. Listen carefully and be prepared to wait in silence for an answer as this can be a constructive way of encouraging the employee to be more forthcoming.

Establish whether the employee is prepared to accept that they may have done something wrong or are not performing to the required standard. Then agree the steps which should be taken to remedy the situation.

If it is not practical for witnesses to attend, consider proceeding if it is clear that their verbal evidence will not affect the substance of the complaint. Alternatively, consider an adjournment to allow questions to be put to a witness who cannot attend in person but who has submitted a witness statement.

General questioning and discussion

You should:

- use this stage to establish all the facts

- ask the employee if they have any explanation for the alleged misconduct or unsatisfactory performance, or if there are any special circumstances to be taken into account

- if it becomes clear during this stage that the employee has provided an adequate explanation or there is no real evidence to support the allegation, bring the proceedings to a close

- keep the approach formal and polite and encourage the employee to speak freely with a view to establishing the facts. A properly conducted disciplinary meeting should be a two-way process. Use questions to clarify the issues and to check that what has been said is understood. Ask open-ended questions, for example, 'what happened then?' to get the broad picture. Ask precise, closed questions requiring a yes/no answer only when specific information is needed

- do not get involved in arguments and do not make personal or humiliating remarks. Avoid physical contact or gestures which could be misinterpreted or misconstrued as judgemental.

If new facts emerge, it may be necessary to adjourn the meeting to investigate them and reconvene the meeting when this has been done.

2

Summing up

Summarise the main points of the discussion after questioning is completed. This allows all parties to be reminded of the nature of the offence, the arguments and evidence put forward and to ensure nothing is missed. Ask the employee if they have anything further to say. This should help to demonstrate to the employee that they have been treated reasonably.

Adjournment before decision

Adjourn before a decision is taken about whether a disciplinary penalty is appropriate. This allows time for reflection and proper consideration. It also allows for any further checking of any matters raised, particularly if there is any dispute over facts.

What problems may arise and how should they be handled?

Extract: Acas Code of Practice on disciplinary and grievance procedures

Where an employee raises a grievance during a disciplinary process the disciplinary process may be temporarily suspended in order to deal with the grievance. Where the grievance and disciplinary cases are related, it may be appropriate to deal with both issues concurrently.

When an employee raises a grievance during the meeting it may sometimes be appropriate to consider stopping the meeting and suspending the disciplinary procedure – for example when:

- the grievance relates to a conflict of interest that the manager holding the disciplinary meeting is alleged to have

- bias is alleged in the conduct of the disciplinary meeting

- management have been selective in the evidence they have supplied to the manager holding the meeting

- there is possible discrimination.

It would not be appropriate to suspend the meeting where the employee makes an invalid point. For example if they mistakenly claim that they have the right to be legally represented or that a collectively agreed and applicable procedure does not apply to them because they are not a union member.

It is possible that the disciplinary meeting may not proceed smoothly – people may be upset or angry. If the employee becomes upset or distressed allow time for them to regain composure before continuing. If the distress is too great to continue then adjourn and reconvene at a later date – however, the issues should not be avoided. Clearly during the meeting there may be some 'letting off steam', and this can be helpful in finding out what has actually happened. However, abusive language or conduct should not be tolerated.

Allow the employee to be accompanied at the meeting

Extract: Acas Code of Practice on disciplinary and grievance procedures

Workers have a statutory right to be accompanied by a companion where the disciplinary meeting could result in:

- a formal warning being issued; or

- the taking of some other disciplinary action; or

- the confirmation of a warning or some other disciplinary action (appeal hearings).

The statutory right is to be accompanied by a fellow worker, a trade union representative, or an official employed by a trade union. A trade union representative who is not an employed official must have been certified by their union as being competent to accompany a worker. Employers must agree to a worker's request to be accompanied by any companion from one of these categories. Workers may also alter their choice of companion if they wish. As a matter of good practice, in making their choice workers should bear in mind the practicalities of the arrangements. For instance, a worker may choose to be accompanied by a companion who is suitable, willing and available on site rather than someone from a geographically remote location.

To exercise the statutory right to be accompanied workers must make a reasonable request. What is reasonable will depend on the circumstances of each individual case. A request to be accompanied does not have to be in writing or within a certain time frame. However, a worker should provide enough time for the employer to deal with the companion's attendance at the meeting. Workers should also consider how they make their request so that it is clearly understood, for instance by letting the employer know in advance the name of the companion where possible and whether they are a fellow worker or trade union official or representative.

If a worker's chosen companion will not be available at the time proposed for the hearing by the employer, the employer must postpone the hearing to a time proposed by the worker provided that the alternative time is both reasonable and not more than five working days after the date originally proposed.

The companion should be allowed to address the hearing to put and sum up the worker's case, respond on behalf of the worker to any views expressed at the meeting and confer with the worker during the hearing. The companion does not, however, have the right to answer questions on the worker's behalf, address the hearing if the worker does not wish it or prevent the employer from explaining their case.

What is the right to be accompanied?

Workers have a statutory right to be accompanied where they are required or invited by their employer to attend certain disciplinary or grievance meetings. The chosen companion may be a fellow worker, a trade union representative, or an official employed by a trade union. A trade union representative who is not an employed official must have been certified by their union as being competent to accompany a worker. Workers must make a reasonable request to their employer to be accompanied.

When does the right apply?

Employees have the right to be accompanied at meetings that could result in:

- a formal warning being issued to a worker (ie a warning that will be placed on the worker's record);

- the taking of some other disciplinary action (such as suspension without pay, demotion or dismissal) or other action; or

- the confirmation of a warning or some other disciplinary action (such as an appeal hearing).

Informal discussions, counselling sessions or investigatory meetings do not attract the right to be accompanied. Meetings to investigate an issue are not disciplinary meetings. If it becomes apparent that formal disciplinary action may be needed then this should be dealt with at a formal meeting at which the employee will have the statutory right to be accompanied.

What is a reasonable request?

Whether a request for a companion is reasonable will depend on the circumstances of the individual case and, ultimately, it is a matter for the courts and tribunals to decide (Refer to Appendix 6 which outlines important changes to making Employment tribunal claims). However, a worker should provide enough time for the employer to deal with the companion's attendance at the meeting. Workers should also consider how they make their request so that it is clearly understood, for instance by letting the employer know in advance the name of the companion where possible and whether they are a fellow worker or trade union official or representative.

The companion

The companion may be:

- a fellow worker (ie another of the employer's workers)

- an official employed by a trade union

- a workplace trade union representative, as long as they have been reasonably certified in writing by their union as having experience of, or having received training in, acting as a worker's companion at disciplinary or grievance hearings. Certification may take the form of a card or letter.

Employers are free, but are not obliged, to allow workers to be accompanied by a companion who does not fall within the above categories. Some workers may have a contractual right to be accompanied by persons other than those listed above (for instance a professional support body, partner, spouse or legal representative).

Reasonable adjustment may be needed for a worker with a disability (and possibly for their companion if they are disabled). For example the provision of a support worker or advocate with knowledge of the disability and its effects.

Workers may ask an official from any trade union to accompany them at a disciplinary or grievance hearing, regardless of whether or not they are a member or the union is recognised.

Fellow workers or trade union officials do not have to accept a request to accompany a worker, and they should not be pressurised to do so.

Trade unions should ensure that their officials are trained in the role of acting as a worker's companion. Even when a trade union official has experience of acting in the role, there may still be a need for periodic refresher training. Employers should consider allowing time off for this training.

A worker who has agreed to accompany a colleague employed by the same employer is entitled to take a reasonable amount of paid time off to fulfil that responsibility. This should cover the hearing and it is also good practice to allow time for the companion to familiarise themselves with the case and confer with the worker before and after the hearing.

A lay trade union official is permitted to take a reasonable amount of paid time off to accompany a worker at a hearing, as long as the worker is employed by the same employer. In cases where a lay official agrees to accompany a worker employed by another organisation, time off is a matter for agreement by the parties concerned.

Applying the right

The employer should allow a companion to have a say about the date and time of a hearing. If the companion cannot attend on a proposed date, the worker can suggest an alternative time and date so long as it is reasonable and it is not more than five working days after the original date.

Before the hearing takes place, the worker should tell the employer who they have chosen as a companion. In certain circumstances (for instance when the companion is an official of a non-recognised trade union) it can be helpful for the companion and employer to make contact before the hearing.

The companion should be allowed to address the hearing in order to:

- put the worker's case

- sum up the worker's case

- respond on the worker's behalf to any view expressed at the hearing.

The companion can also confer with the worker during the hearing. It is good practice to allow the companion to participate as fully as possible in the hearing, including asking witnesses questions. The employer is, however, not legally required to permit the companion to answer questions on the worker's behalf, or to address the hearing if the worker does not

Taking action after the disciplinary meeting

Extract: Acas Code of Practice on disciplinary and grievance procedures

After the meeting decide whether or not disciplinary or any other action is justified and inform the employee accordingly in writing.

Where misconduct is confirmed or the employee is found to be performing unsatisfactorily it is usual to give the employee a written warning. A further act of misconduct or failure to improve performance within a set period would normally result in a final written warning.

If an employee's first misconduct or unsatisfactory performance is sufficiently serious, it may be appropriate to move directly to a final written warning. This might occur where the employee's actions have had, or are liable to have, a serious or harmful impact on the organisation.

A first or final written warning should set out the nature of the misconduct or poor performance and the change in behaviour or improvement in performance required (with timescale). The employee should be told how long the warning will remain current. The employee should be informed of the consequences of further misconduct, or failure to improve performance, within the set period following a final warning. For instance that it may result in dismissal or some other contractual penalty such as demotion or loss of seniority.

A decision to dismiss should only be taken by a manager who has the authority to do so. The employee should be informed as soon as possible of the reasons for the dismissal, the date on which the employment contract will end, the appropriate period of notice and their right of appeal.

Some acts, termed gross misconduct, are so serious in themselves or have such serious consequences that they may call for dismissal without notice for a first offence. But a fair disciplinary process, should always be followed, before dismissing for gross misconduct.

Disciplinary rules should give examples of acts which the employer regards as acts of gross misconduct. These may vary according to the nature of the organisation and what it does, but might include things such as theft or fraud, physical violence, gross negligence or serious insubordination.

Where an employee is persistently unable or unwilling to attend a disciplinary meeting without good cause the employer should make a decision on the evidence available.

wish it, or to prevent the employer from explaining their case.

Workers whose employers fail to comply with a reasonable request to be accompanied may present a complaint to an employment tribunal. Workers may also complain to a tribunal if employers fail to re-arrange a hearing to a reasonable date proposed by the worker when a companion cannot attend on the date originally proposed. The tribunal may order compensation of up to two weeks' pay.

It is unlawful to disadvantage workers for using their right to be accompanied or for being companions. This could lead to a claim to an employment tribunal.

If you are (or expect to be) affected by such an issue, see Appendix 6 on important changes to making a tribunal claim.

What should be considered before deciding any disciplinary penalty?

When deciding whether a disciplinary penalty is appropriate and what form it should take, consideration should be given to:

- whether the rules of the organisation indicate what the likely penalty will be as a result of the particular misconduct

- the penalty imposed in similar cases in the past

- whether standards of other employees are acceptable, and that this employee is not being unfairly singled out

- the employee's disciplinary record (including current warnings), general work record, work experience, position and length of service

- any special circumstances which might make it appropriate to adjust the severity of the penalty

- whether the proposed penalty is reasonable in view of all the circumstances

- whether any training, additional support or adjustments to the work are necessary.

It should be clear what the normal organisational practice is for dealing with the kind of misconduct or unsatisfactory performance under consideration. This does not mean that similar offences will always call for the same disciplinary action: each case must be looked at on its own merits and any relevant circumstances taken into account. Such relevant circumstances may include health or domestic problems, provocation, justifiable ignorance of the rule or standard involved or inconsistent treatment in the past.

If guidance is needed on formal disciplinary action, seek advice, where possible, from someone who will not be involved in hearing any potential appeal. Call the Acas helpline on **0300 123 1100** (Open Monday – Friday 8am–8pm & Saturday 9am–1pm) to talk to one of our advisers.

Imposing the disciplinary penalty
First formal action – unsatisfactory performance
In cases of unsatisfactory performance an employee should be given an 'improvement note', setting out:

- the performance problem

- the improvement that is required

- the timescale for achieving this improvement

- a review date and

- any support, including any training, that the employer will provide to assist the employee.

The employee should be informed that the note represents the first stage of a formal procedure and is equivalent to a first written warning and that failure to improve could lead to a final written warning and, ultimately, dismissal. A copy of the note should be kept and used as the basis for monitoring and reviewing performance over a specified period (eg, six months).

If an employee's unsatisfactory performance – or its continuance – is sufficiently serious, for example because it is having, or is likely to have, a serious harmful effect on the organisation, it may be justifiable to move directly to a final written warning.

Discipline in practice 2

A member of staff in accounts makes a number of mistakes on invoices to customers. You bring the mistakes to his attention, make sure he has had the right training and impress on him the need for accuracy but the mistakes continue. You invite the employee to a disciplinary meeting and inform him of his right to be accompanied by a colleague or employee representative. At the meeting the employee does not give a satisfactory explanation for the mistakes so you decide to issue an improvement note setting out: the problem, the improvement required, the timescale for improvement, the support available and a review date. You inform the employee that a failure to improve may lead to a final written warning.

First formal action – misconduct

In cases of misconduct, employees should be given a written warning setting out the nature of the misconduct and the change in behaviour required.

The warning should also inform the employee that a final written warning may be considered if there is further misconduct. A record of the warning should be kept, but it should be disregarded for disciplinary purposes

after a specified period (eg, six months).

Final written warning

If the employee has a current warning about conduct or performance then further misconduct or unsatisfactory performance (whichever is relevant) may warrant a final written warning. This may also be the case where 'first offence' misconduct is sufficiently serious, but would not justify dismissal. Such a warning should normally remain current for a specified period, for example, 12 months, and contain a statement that further misconduct or unsatisfactory performance may lead to dismissal.

Dismissal or other sanction

If the employee has received a final written warning further misconduct or unsatisfactory performance may warrant dismissal. Alternatively the contract may allow for a different disciplinary penalty instead. Such a penalty may include disciplinary transfer, disciplinary suspension without pay[7], demotion, loss of seniority or loss of increment. These sanctions may only be applied if allowed for in the employee's contract or with the employee's agreement.

Any penalty should be confirmed in writing, and the procedure and time limits for appeal set out clearly.

Discipline in practice 3

An employee in a small firm makes a series of mistakes in letters to one of your key customers promising impossible delivery dates. The customer is upset at your firm's failure to meet delivery dates and threatens to take his business elsewhere.

You are the owner of the business and carry out an investigation and invite the employee to a disciplinary meeting. You inform her of her right to be accompanied by a colleague or employee representative.

Example outcome of meeting

At the meeting the employee does not give a satisfactory explanation for the mistakes and admits that her training covered the importance of agreeing realistic delivery dates with her manager. During your investigation, her team leader and section manager told you they had stressed to the employee the importance of agreeing delivery dates with them before informing the customer. In view of the seriousness of the mistakes and the possible impact on the business, you issue the employee with a final written warning. You inform the employee that failure to improve will lead to dismissal and of her right to appeal.

Example outcome of meeting in different circumstances

At the meeting, the employee reveals that her team leader would not let her attend training as the section was too busy. Subsequently the team leader was absent sick and the employee asked the section manager for help with setting delivery dates. The manager said he was too busy and told the employee to 'use her initiative'. Your other investigations support the employee's explanation. You inform the employee that you will not be taking disciplinary action and will make arrangements for her to be properly trained. You decide to carry out a review of general management standards on supervision and training.

There may be occasions when, depending on the seriousness of the misconduct involved, it will be appropriate to consider dismissal without notice (see over).

Dismissal with notice

Employees should only be dismissed if, despite warnings, conduct or performance does not improve to the required level within the specified time period. Dismissal must be reasonable in all the circumstances of the case.

Unless the employee is being dismissed for reasons of gross misconduct, he or she should receive

Discipline in practice 4

A member of your telephone sales team has been to lunch to celebrate success in an exam. He returns from lunch in a very merry mood, is slurring his speech and is evidently not fit to carry out his duties. You decide to send him home and invite him in writing to a disciplinary meeting setting out his alleged behaviour of gross misconduct for which he could be dismissed. Your letter includes information about his right to be accompanied by a colleague or employee representative.

At the meeting he admits he had too much to drink, is very apologetic and promises that such a thing will not happen again. He is one of your most valued members of staff and has an exemplary record over his 10 years service with you. You know that being unfit for work because of excessive alcohol is listed in your company rules as gross misconduct. In view of the circumstances and the employee's record, however, you decide not to dismiss him but give him a final written warning. You inform the employee of his right to appeal.

the appropriate period of notice or payment in lieu of notice.

Dismissal without notice

Employers should give all employees a clear indication of the type of misconduct which, in the light of the requirements of the employer's business, will warrant dismissal without the normal period of notice or pay in lieu of notice. So far as possible the types of offences which fall into this category of 'gross misconduct' should be clearly specified in the rules, although such a list cannot normally be exhaustive.

What is gross misconduct?

Gross misconduct is generally seen as misconduct serious enough to overturn the contract between the employer and the employee thus justifying summary dismissal. Acts which constitute gross misconduct must be very serious and are best determined by organisations in the

light of their own particular circumstances. However, examples of gross misconduct might include:

- theft or fraud

- physical violence or bullying

- deliberate and serious damage to property

- serious misuse of an organisation's property or name

- deliberately accessing internet sites containing pornographic, offensive or obscene material

- serious insubordination

- unlawful discrimination or harassment

- bringing the organisation into serious disrepute

- serious incapability at work brought on by alcohol or illegal drugs

- causing loss, damage or injury through serious negligence

- a serious breach of health and safety rules

- a serious breach of confidence.

If an employer considers an employee guilty of gross misconduct and thus liable for summary dismissal, it is still important to follow a fair procedure as for any other disciplinary offence. This will include establishing the facts of the case before taking any action, holding a meeting with the employee and allowing the employee the right of appeal. It should be made clear to the employee that dismissal is a possibility. A short period of suspension with full pay to help establish the facts or to allow tempers to cool may be helpful. However, such a period of suspension should only be imposed after careful consideration and should be kept under review. It should be made clear to the employee that the suspension is not

a disciplinary action and does not involve any prejudgement.

How should the employee be informed of the disciplinary decision?

Details of any disciplinary action should be given in writing to the employee as soon as the decision is made. See example letters at Appendix 3. A copy of the notification should be retained by the employer. The written notification should specify:

- the nature of the misconduct

- any period of time given for improvement and the improvement expected

- the disciplinary penalty and, where appropriate, how long it will last

- the likely consequences of further misconduct

- the timescale for lodging an appeal and how it should be made.

The organisation may wish to require the employee to acknowledge receipt of the written notification.

Written reasons for dismissal

Employees with two years' service or more have the right to request a 'written statement of reasons for dismissal'. Employers are required by law to comply within 14 days of the request being made, unless it is not reasonably practicable. It is good practice to give written reasons for all dismissals.

A woman who is dismissed during pregnancy or maternity or adoption leave is automatically entitled to the written statement without having to request it and irrespective of length of service[8].

The written statement can be used in evidence in any subsequent Tribunal proceedings, for example, in relation to a complaint of unfair dismissal. Refer to Appendix 6 which outlines important changes to making Employment tribunal claims.

Time limits for warnings

Except in agreed special circumstances, any disciplinary action taken should be disregarded for disciplinary purposes after a specified period of satisfactory conduct or performance. This period should be established clearly when the disciplinary procedure is being drawn up. A decision to dismiss should not be based on an expired warning but the fact that there is an expired warning may explain why the employer does not substitute a lesser sanction.

Normal practice is for different types of warnings to remain in force for different periods. For example, a first written warning might be valid for up to six months while a final written warning may remain in force for 12 months (or more in exceptional circumstances). Warnings should cease to be 'live' following the specified period of satisfactory conduct.

There may be occasions where an employee's conduct is satisfactory throughout the period the warning is in force, only to lapse very soon thereafter. Where a pattern emerges and/or there is evidence of abuse, the employee's disciplinary record should be borne in mind in deciding how long any warning should last.

2

Provide employees with an opportunity to appeal

> **Extract: Acas Code of Practice on disciplinary and grievance procedures**
>
> Where an employee feels that disciplinary action taken against them is wrong or unjust they should appeal against the decision. Appeals should be heard without unreasonable delay and ideally at an agreed time and place. Employees should let employers know the grounds for their appeal in writing.
>
> The appeal should be dealt with impartially and wherever possible, by a manager who has not previously been involved in the case.
>
> Workers have a statutory right to be accompanied at appeal hearings.
>
> Employees should be informed in writing of the results of the appeal hearing as soon as possible.

The opportunity to appeal against a disciplinary decision is essential to natural justice, and appeals may be raised by employees on any number of grounds, for instance new evidence, undue severity or inconsistency of the penalty. The appeal may either be a review of the disciplinary sanction or a re-hearing depending on the grounds of the appeal.

An appeal must never be used as an opportunity to punish the employee for appealing the original decision, and it should not result in any increase in penalty as this may deter individuals from appealing.

What should an appeals procedure contain?

It should:

- specify a time-limit within which the appeal should be lodged (five working days is commonly felt appropriate although this may be extended in particular circumstances)

- provide for appeals to be dealt with speedily, particularly those involving suspension or dismissal

- wherever possible provide for the appeal to be heard by someone senior in authority to the person who took the disciplinary decision and, if possible, someone who was not involved in the original meeting or decision

- spell out what action may be taken by those hearing the appeal

- set out the right to be accompanied at any appeal meeting

- provide that the employee, or a companion if the employee so wishes, has an opportunity to comment on any new evidence arising during the appeal before any decision is taken.

Small organisations
In small organisations, even if there is no more senior manager available, another manager should, if possible, hear the appeal. If this is not possible consider whether the owner or, in the case of a charity, the board of trustees, should hear the appeal. Whoever hears the appeal should consider it as impartially as possible.

How should an appeal hearing be conducted? Before the appeal ensure that the individual knows when and where it is to be held, and of their statutory right to be accompanied (see p23). Hold the meeting in a place which will be free from interruptions. Make sure the relevant records and notes of the original meeting are available for all concerned. See sample letters at Appendix 3.

At the meeting
You should:

- introduce those present to each other, explaining their presence if necessary

- explain the purpose of the meeting, how it will be conducted, and the powers the person/people hearing the appeal have

- ask the employee why he or she is appealing

- pay particular attention to any new evidence that has been introduced, and ensure the employee has the opportunity to comment on it

- once the relevant issues have been thoroughly explored, summarise the facts and call an adjournment to consider the decision

- change a previous decision if it becomes apparent that it was not soundly based – such action does not undermine authority but rather makes clear the independent nature of the appeal. If the decision is overturned consider whether training for managers needs to be improved, if rules need clarification, or are if there other implications to be considered?

- inform the employee of the results of the appeal and the reasons for the decision and confirm it in writing. Make it clear, if this is the case, that this decision is final. See sample letters at Appendix 3.

Dealing with special cases

Extract: Acas Code of Practice on disciplinary and grievance procedures

Where disciplinary action is being considered against an employee who is a trade union representative the normal disciplinary procedure should be followed. Depending on the circumstances, however, it is advisable to discuss the matter at an early stage with an official employed by the union, after obtaining the employee's agreement.

If an employee is charged with, or convicted of a criminal offence this is not normally in itself reason for disciplinary action. Consideration needs to be given to what effect the charge or conviction has on the employee's suitability to do the job and their relationship with their employer, work colleagues and customers.

Trade union officials

Although normal disciplinary standards apply to their conduct as employees, disciplinary action against a trade union representative can be construed as an attack on the union if not handled carefully (see also p19).

Criminal charges or convictions

An employee should not be dismissed or otherwise disciplined solely because he or she has been charged with or convicted of a criminal offence. The question to be asked in such cases is whether the employee's conduct or conviction merits action because of its employment implications.

Where it is thought the conduct warrants disciplinary action the following guidance should be borne in mind:

- the employer should investigate the facts as far as possible, come to a view about them and consider whether the conduct is sufficiently serious to warrant instituting the disciplinary procedure

- where the conduct requires prompt attention the employer need not await the outcome of the prosecution before taking fair and reasonable action

- where the police are called in they should not be asked to conduct any investigation on behalf of the employer, nor should they be present at any meeting or disciplinary meeting.

In some cases the nature of the alleged offence may not justify disciplinary action – for example, off-duty conduct which has no bearing on employment – but the employee may not be available for work because he or she is in custody or on remand. In these cases employers should decide whether, in the light of the needs of the organisation, the employee's job can be held open. Where a criminal conviction leads, for example, to the loss of a licence so that continued employment in a particular job would be illegal, employers should consider whether alternative work is appropriate and available.

Where an employee, charged with or convicted of a criminal offence, refuses or is unable to cooperate with the employer's disciplinary investigations and proceedings, this should not deter an employer from taking action. The employee should be advised in writing that unless further information is provided, a disciplinary decision will be taken on the basis of the information available and could result in dismissal.

Where there is little likelihood of an employee returning to employment, it may be argued that the contract of employment has been terminated through 'frustration'[9]. However, the doctrine is normally accepted by the courts only where the frustrating event renders all performance of the employment contract clearly impossible. It is normally better for the employer to take disciplinary action.

An employee who has been charged with, or convicted of, a criminal offence may become unacceptable to colleagues, resulting in workforce pressure to dismiss and threats of industrial action. Employers should bear in mind that they may have to justify the reasonableness of any decision to dismiss and that an employment tribunal will ignore threats of, and actual industrial action when determining the fairness of a decision (Section 107, Employment Rights Act 1996). They should consider all relevant factors, not just disruption to production, before reaching a reasonable decision. If you are (or expect to be) affected by such an issue, see Appendix 6 on important changes to making a tribunal claim.

Use of external consultants

In some instances employers may wish to bring in external consultants to carry out an investigation. Employers will still be responsible for any inappropriate or discriminatory behaviour if the investigation is carried out by consultants. Make arrangements for the investigation to be overseen by a representative of management. Make sure that the consultants follow the organisation's disciplinary policies and procedures and deal with the case fairly in accordance with the Acas Code of Practice.

Employees to whom the full procedure is not immediately available

It may be sensible to arrange time off with pay so that employees who are in isolated locations or on shifts can attend a disciplinary meeting on the main site in normal working hours. Alternatively, if a number of witnesses need to attend it may be better to hold the disciplinary meeting on the nightshift or at the particular location.

Grievances

Keys to handling grievances in the workplace

Grievances *Keys to handling grievances in the workplace*

Resolve grievances informally

In organisations where managers have an open policy for communication and consultation problems and concerns are often raised and settled as a matter of course.

Employees should aim to settle most grievances informally with their line manager. Many problems can be raised and settled during the course of everyday working relationships. This also allows for problems to be settled quickly.

In some cases outside help such as an independent mediator can help resolve problems especially those involving working relationships. See p7 for more information.

Dealing rules and procedures

Extract: Acas Code of Practice on disciplinary and grievance procedures

Fairness and transparency are promoted by developing and using rules and procedures for handling disciplinary and grievance situations. These should be set down in writing, be specific and clear. Employees and, where appropriate, their representatives should be involved in the development of rules and procedures. It is also important to help employees and managers understand what the rules and procedures are, where they can be found and how they are to be used.

What is a grievance and why have a procedure?

Extract: Acas Code of Practice on disciplinary and grievance procedures

Grievances are concerns, problems or complaints that employees raise with their employers.

Anybody working in an organisation may, at some time, have problems or concerns about their work, working conditions or relationships with colleagues that they wish to talk about with management. They want the grievance to be addressed, and if possible, resolved. It is also clearly in management's interests to resolve problems before they can develop into major difficulties for all concerned.

Issues that may cause grievances include:

● terms and conditions of employment

● health and safety

● work relations

● bullying and harassment

● new working practices

● working environment

● organisational change

● discrimination.

Grievances may occur at all levels and the Acas Code of Practice, and this guidance, applies equally to management and employees.

A written procedure can help clarify the process and help to ensure that employees are aware of their rights such as to be accompanied at grievance meetings (see p47 on the right to be accompanied). Some

organisations use, or may wish to use, external mediators to help resolve grievances (see p7). Where this is the case the procedure should explain how and when mediators may be used.

Employees might raise issues about matters not entirely within the control of the organisation, such as client or customer relationships (for instance where an employee is working on another employer's site). These should be treated in the same way as grievances within the organisation, with the employer/manager investigating as far as possible and taking action if required. The organisation should make it very clear to any third party that grievances are taken seriously and action will be taken to protect their employees.

Extract: Acas Code of Practice on disciplinary and grievance procedures

The provisions of this Code do not apply to grievances raised on behalf of two or more employees by a representative of a recognised trade union or other appropriate workplace representative. These grievances should be handled in accordance with the organisation's collective grievance process.

Occasionally a collective grievance may arise where a number of people have the same grievance at the same time. If there is a grievance which applies to more than one person this should be resolved in accordance with the organisation's collective grievance process – where one exists.

Training for dealing with grievances

Management and employee representatives who may be involved in grievance matters should be trained for the task. They should be familiar with the provisions of the grievance procedure, and know how to conduct or represent at grievance hearings. Consideration might be given to training managers and employee representatives jointly. For information about suitable training see the Acas website at www.acas.org.uk/training.

Keeping written records

What records should be kept?

The foreword to the Code of Practice advises employers to keep a written record of any disciplinary or grievances cases they deal with.

Records should include:

- the nature of the grievance

- what was decided and actions taken

- the reason for the actions

- whether an appeal was lodged

- the outcome of the appeal

- any subsequent developments.

Records should be treated as confidential and be kept no longer than necessary in accordance with the Data Protection Act 1998. This Act gives individuals the right to request and have access to certain personal data. The Information Commissioner has produced Codes of Practice covering recruitment and selection, employment records, monitoring at work and information about an employee's health[10].

Copies of meeting records should be given to the employee including copies of any formal minutes that may have been taken. In certain circumstances (for example to protect a witness) the employer might withhold some information.

Dealing with formal grievances

Extract: Acas Code of Practice on disciplinary and grievance procedures*

Where some form of formal action is needed, what action is reasonable or justified will depend on all the circumstances of the particular case. Employment tribunals will take the size and resources of an employer into account when deciding on relevant cases and it may sometimes not be practicable for all employers to take all of the steps set out in this Code.

That said, whenever a disciplinary or grievance process is being followed it is important to deal with issues fairly. There are a number of elements to this:

- Employers and employees should raise and deal with issues **promptly** and should not unreasonably delay meetings, decisions or confirmation of those decisions.

- Employers and employees should act **consistently**.

- Employers should carry out any necessary **investigations**, to establish the facts of the case.

- Employers should **inform** employees of the basis of the problem and give them an opportunity to **put their case** in response before any decisions are made.

- Employers should allow employees to be **accompanied** at any formal disciplinary or grievance meeting.

- Employers should allow an employee to **appeal** against any formal decision made.

*Refer to Appendix 6 which outlines important changes to making Employment Tribunal claims.

The following pages give detailed guidance on handling formal grievances. Always bear in mind the need for fairness when following procedures, taking account of the elements from the Acas Code of Practice reproduced above.

Let the employer know the nature of the grievance

Where a grievance is serious or an employee has attempted to raise a problem informally without success, the employee should raise it formally with management in writing.

Where employees have difficulty expressing themselves because of language or other difficulties they may like to seek help from trade union or other employee representatives or from colleagues.

When stating their grievance, employees should stick to the facts and avoid language which may be considered insulting or abusive.

Where the grievance is against the line manager the employee may approach another manager or raise the issue with their HR department if there is one. It is helpful if the grievance procedure sets out who the individual should approach in these circumstances.

In small firms run by an owner/manager there will be no alternative manager to raise a grievance with. It is in the interests of such employers to make it clear that they will treat all grievances fairly and objectively even if the grievance is about something they have said or done.

Holding a grievance meeting

What is a grievance meeting?

In general terms a grievance meeting deals with any grievance raised by an employee. For the purposes of the legal right to be accompanied, a grievance meeting is defined as a meeting where an employer deals with a complaint about a 'duty owed by them to a worker' (see p47).

Preparing for the meeting
Managers should:

- arrange a meeting, ideally within five working days, in private where there will not be interruptions

- consider arranging for someone who is not involved in the case to take a note of the meeting and to act as a witness to what was said

- whether similar grievances have been raised before, how they have been resolved, and any follow-up action that has been necessary. This allows consistency of treatment

- consider arranging for an interpreter where the employee has difficulty speaking English

- consider whether any reasonable adjustments are necessary for a person who is disabled and/or their companion

- consider whether to offer independent mediation – see p7.

Conduct of the meeting
Managers should:

- remember that a grievance hearing is not the same as a disciplinary hearing, and is an occasion when discussion and dialogue may lead to an amicable solution

- make introductions as necessary

- invite the employee to re-state their grievance and how they would like to see it resolved

- put care and thought into resolving grievances. They are not normally issues calling for snap decisions, and the employee may have been holding the grievance for a long time. Make allowances for any reasonable 'letting off steam' if the employee is under stress

- consider adjourning the meeting if it is necessary to investigate any new facts which arise

- sum up the main points

- tell the employee when they might reasonably expect a response if one cannot be made at the time, bearing in mind the time limits set out in the organisation's procedure.

Be calm, fair and follow the procedure
In smaller organisations, grievances can sometimes be taken as personal criticism – employers should be careful to hear any grievance in a calm and objective manner, being as fair to the employee as possible in the resolution of the problem. Following the grievance procedure can make this easier.

3

Grievances in practice 1

You are the owner of a small firm. An employee has been complaining that she is being given too much work and can't complete it in time. You have told the employee that her predecessor had no problem completing the same amount of work and that things will get easier with experience. The employee is not happy and puts her grievance to you in writing.

You invite the employee to a meeting to discuss the grievance and inform her of her right to be accompanied. At the meeting you discover that the employee is working on a different computer from her predecessor. The computer is slower and uses an old version of the software required to carry out the work. You agree to upgrade the software, provide training and to review progress in a month. You confirm what was agreed in writing and inform the employee of her right to an appeal meeting if she feels her grievance has not been satisfactorily resolved.

Grievances about fellow employees

These can be made easier by following the grievance procedure. An employee may be the cause of grievances among his or her co-employees – perhaps on grounds of personal hygiene, attitude, or capability for the job. Employers must deal with these cases carefully and should generally start by talking privately to the individual about the concerns of fellow employees. This may resolve the grievance. Alternatively, if those involved are willing, an independent mediator may be able to help (see p7). Care needs to be taken that any discussion with someone being complained about does not turn into a meeting at which they would be entitled to be accompanied (see p47).

Allow the employee to be accompanied at the meeting

Extract: Acas Code of Practice on disciplinary and grievance procedures

Workers have a statutory right to be accompanied by a companion at a grievance meeting which deals with a complaint about a duty owed by the employer to the worker. So this would apply where the complaint is, for example, that the employer is not honouring the worker's contract, or is in breach of legislation.

The statutory right is to be accompanied by a fellow worker, a trade union representative, or an official employed by a trade union. A trade union representative who is not an employed official must have been certified by their union as being competent to accompany a worker. Employers must agree to a worker's request to be accompanied by any companion from one of these categories. Workers may also alter their choice of companion if they wish. As a matter of good practice, in making their choice workers should bear in mind the practicalities of the arrangements. For instance, a worker may choose to be accompanied by a companion who is suitable, willing and available on site rather than someone from a geographically remote location.

To exercise the statutory right to be accompanied workers must make a reasonable request. What is reasonable will depend on the circumstances of each individual case. A request to be accompanied does not have to be in writing or within a certain time frame. However, a worker should provide enough time for the employer to deal with the companion's attendance at the meeting. Workers should also consider how they make their request so that it is clearly understood, for instance by letting the employer know in advance the name of the companion where possible and whether they are a fellow worker or trade union official or representative.

If a worker's chosen companion will not be available at the time proposed for the hearing by the employer, the employer must postpone the hearing to a time proposed by the worker provided that the alternative time is both reasonable and not more than five working days after the date originally proposed.

The companion should be allowed to address the hearing to put and sum up the worker's case, respond on behalf of the worker to any views expressed at the meeting and confer with the worker during the hearing. The companion does not, however, have the right to answer questions on the worker's behalf, address the hearing if the worker does not wish it or prevent the employer from explaining their case.

3

When do workers have the right to be accompanied?

For the purposes of this right, a grievance hearing is a meeting at which an employer deals with a complaint about a duty owed by them to a worker, whether the duty arises from statute or common law (for example contractual commitments).

For instance, an individual's request for a pay rise is unlikely to fall within the definition, unless a right to an increase is specifically provided for in the contract or the request raises an issue about equal pay. Equally, most employers will be under no legal duty to provide their workers with car parking facilities, and a grievance about such facilities would carry no right to be accompanied at a hearing by a companion. However, if a worker were disabled and needed a car to get to and from work, they probably would be entitled to a companion at a grievance hearing, as an issue might arise as to whether the employer was meeting their obligations under the Equality Act 2010.

It is generally good practice to allow workers to be accompanied at a formal grievance meeting even when the statutory right does not apply.

What is a reasonable request?

Whether a request for a companion is reasonable will depend on the circumstances of the individual case and, ultimately, it is a matter for the courts and tribunals to decide. However, a worker should provide enough time for the employer to deal with the companion's attendance at the meeting. Workers should also consider how they make their request so that it is clearly understood, for instance by letting the employer know in advance the name of the companion where possible and whether they are a fellow worker or trade union official or representative.

The companion

The companion may be:

- a fellow worker (ie another of the employer's workers)

- an official employed by a trade union

- a workplace trade union representative, as long as they have been reasonably certified in writing by their union as having experience of, or having received training in, acting as a worker's companion at disciplinary or grievance hearings. Certification may take the form of a card or letter.

Employers are free, but are not obliged, to allow workers to be accompanied by a companion who does not fall within the above categories. Some workers may have a contractual right to be accompanied by persons other than those listed above (for instance a professional support body, partner, spouse or legal representative).

Reasonable adjustment may be needed for a worker with a disability (and possibly for their companion if they are disabled). For example the provision of a support worker or advocate with knowledge of the disability and its effects.

Workers may ask an official from any trade union to accompany them at a disciplinary or grievance hearing, regardless of whether or not they are a member or the union is recognised.

Fellow workers or trade union officials do not have to accept a request to accompany a worker, and they should not be pressurised to do so.

Trade unions should ensure that their officials are trained in the role of acting as a worker's companion. Even when a trade union official has experience of acting in the role, there may still be a need for periodic refresher training. Employers should consider allowing time off for this training.

A worker who has agreed to accompany a colleague employed by the same employer is entitled to take a reasonable amount of paid time off to fulfil that responsibility. This should cover the hearing and it is also good practice to allow time for the companion to familiarise themselves with the case and confer with the worker before and after the hearing. A lay trade union official is permitted to take a reasonable amount of paid time off to accompany a worker at a hearing, as long as the worker is employed by the same employer. In cases where a lay official agrees to accompany a worker employed by another organisation, time off is a matter for agreement by the parties concerned.

Applying the right

Where possible, the employer should allow a companion to have a say in the date and time of a hearing. If the companion cannot attend on a proposed date, the worker can suggest an alternative time and date so long as it is reasonable and it is not more than five working days after the original date.

Before the hearing takes place, the worker should tell the employer who they have chosen as a companion. In certain circumstances (for instance when the companion is an official of a non-recognised trade union) it can be helpful for the companion and employer to make contact before the hearing.

The companion should be allowed to address the meeting in order to:

- put the worker's case

- sum up the worker's case

3

- respond on the worker's behalf to any view expressed at the hearing

- confer with the worker during the meeting.

The companion can also confer with the worker during the hearing. It is good practice to allow the companion to participate as fully as possible in the hearing, including asking witnesses questions. The employer is, however, not legally required to permit the companion to answer questions on the worker's behalf, or to address the hearing if the worker does not wish it, or to prevent the employer from explaining their case.

Workers whose employers fail to comply with a reasonable request to be accompanied may present a complaint to an employment tribunal. Workers may also complain to a tribunal if employers fail to re-arrange a hearing to a reasonable date proposed by the worker when a companion cannot attend on the date originally proposed. The tribunal may order compensation of up to two weeks' pay.

Employers should be careful not to disadvantage workers for using their right to be accompanied or for being companions, as this is against the law and could lead to a claim to an employment tribunal.

If you are (or expect to be) affected by such an issue, see Appendix 6 on important changes to making a tribunal claim.

Decide on appropriate action

Extract: Acas Code of Practice on disciplinary and grievance procedures

Following the meeting decide on what action, if any, to take. Decisions should be communicated to the employee, in writing, without unreasonable delay and, where appropriate, should set out what action the employer intends to take to resolve the grievance. The employee should be informed that they can appeal if they are not content with the action taken.

It is generally good practice to adjourn a meeting before a decision is taken about how to deal with an employee's grievance. This allows time for reflection and proper consideration. It also allows for any further checking of any matters raised.

Set out clearly in writing any action that is to be taken and the employee's right of appeal. Where an employee's grievance is not upheld make sure the reasons are carefully explained.

Bear in mind that actions taken to resolve a grievance may have an impact on other individuals, who may also feel aggrieved.

If the grievance highlights any issues concerning policies, procedures or conduct (even if not sufficiently serious to merit separate disciplinary procedures) they should be addressed as soon as possible.

Ensure any action taken is monitored and reviewed, as appropriate, so that it deals effectively with the issues.

Allow the employee to take the grievance further if not resolved

Extract: Acas Code of Practice on disciplinary and grievance procedures

Where an employee feels that their grievance has not been satisfactorily resolved they should appeal. They should let their employer know the grounds for their appeal without unreasonable delay and in writing.

Appeals should be heard without unreasonable delay and at a time and place which should be notified to the employee in advance.

The appeal should be dealt with impartially and wherever possible by a manager who has not previously been involved in the case.

Workers have a statutory right to be accompanied at any such appeal hearing.

The outcome of the appeal should be communicated to the employee in writing without unreasonable delay.

3

Arranging an appeal

If an employee informs the employer that they are unhappy with the decision after a grievance meeting, the employer should arrange an appeal. As far as reasonably practicable the appeal should be with a more senior manager than the one who dealt with the original grievance.

In small organisations, even if there is no more senior manager available, another manager should, if possible, hear the appeal. If this is not possible consider whether the owner or, in the case of a charity, the board of trustees, should hear the appeal. Whoever hears the appeal should consider it as impartially as possible.

At the same time as inviting the employee to attend the appeal, the employer should remind them of their right to be accompanied at the appeal meeting.

As with the first meeting, the employer should write to the employee with a decision on their grievance as soon as possible. They should also tell the employee if the appeal meeting is the final stage of the grievance procedure.

Large organisations may wish to allow a further appeal to a higher level of management, such as a director. However, in smaller firms the first appeal will usually mark the end of the grievance procedure. Sample grievance procedure (small organisation) is at Appendix 2.

Dealing with special cases

The foreword to the Code of Practice points out that organisations may wish to consider dealing with issues involving bullying, harassment[11] or whistleblowing under a separate procedure. For further advice about how to deal with bullying and harassment see the Acas advice leaflet Bullying and harassment at work: a guide for managers and employers available to order or download from the Acas website www.acas.org.uk/publications.

Clearly confidentiality is of prime importance when handling any such grievance, although the outcome may need to be made known if, for instance, someone is found to have bullied or harassed an individual and the result is disciplinary action. Mediation may be particularly useful in these types of cases see p7.

The
Appendices

Appendix 1 *Disciplinary rules for small organisations*

Checklist

As a minimum, rules should:

- be simple, clear and in writing

- be displayed prominently in the workplace

- be known and understood by all employees

- cover issues such as absences, timekeeping, health and safety and use of organisational facilities and equipment (add any other items relevant to your organisation)

- indicate examples of the type of conduct which will normally lead to disciplinary action other than dismissal – for instance lateness or unauthorised absence

- indicate examples of the type of conduct which will normally lead to dismissal without notice – examples may include working dangerously, stealing or fighting – although much will depend on the circumstances of each offence.

Appendix 2 *Sample disciplinary and grievance procedures*

Sample disciplinary procedure (any organisation)

1. Purpose and scope
This procedure is designed to help and encourage all employees to achieve and maintain standards of conduct, attendance and job performance. The company rules (a copy of which is displayed in the office) and this procedure apply to all employees. The aim is to ensure consistent and fair treatment for all in the organisation.

2. Principles
Informal action will be considered, where appropriate, to resolve problems.

No disciplinary action will be taken against an employee until the case has been fully investigated.

For formal action the employee will be advised of the nature of the complaint against him or her and will be given the opportunity to state his or her case before any decision is made at a disciplinary meeting.

Employees will be provided, where appropriate, with written copies of evidence and relevant witness statements in advance of a disciplinary meeting.

At all stages of the procedure the employee will have the right to be accompanied by a trade union representative, or work colleague.

No employee will be dismissed for a first breach of discipline except in the case of gross misconduct, when the penalty will be dismissal without notice or payment in lieu of notice.

An employee will have the right to appeal against any disciplinary action.

The procedure may be implemented at any stage if the employee's alleged misconduct warrants this.

3. The Procedure
First stage of formal procedure
This will normally be either:

- *an improvement note for unsatisfactory performance* if performance does not meet acceptable standards. This will set out the performance problem, the improvement that is required, the timescale, any help that may be

- given and the right of appeal. The individual will be advised that it constitutes the first stage of the formal procedure. A record of the improvement note will be kept for ... months, but will then be considered spent – subject to achieving and sustaining satisfactory performance

or

- *a first warning for misconduct* if conduct does not meet acceptable standards. This will be in writing and set out the nature of the misconduct and the change in behaviour required and the right of appeal. The warning will also inform the employee that a final written warning may be considered if there is no sustained satisfactory improvement or change. A record of the warning will be kept, but it will be disregarded for disciplinary purposes after a specified period (eg, six months).

Final written warning
If the offence is sufficiently serious, or if there is further misconduct or a failure to improve performance during the currency of a prior warning, a final written warning may be given to the employee. This will give details of the complaint, the improvement required and the timescale. It will also warn that failure to improve may lead to dismissal (or

some other action short of dismissal) and will refer to the right of appeal. A copy of this written warning will be kept by the supervisor but will be disregarded for disciplinary purposes after ... months subject to achieving and sustaining satisfactory conduct or performance.

Dismissal or other sanction
If there is still further misconduct or failure to improve performance the final step in the procedure may be dismissal or some other action short of dismissal such as demotion or disciplinary suspension or transfer (as allowed in the contract of employment). Dismissal decisions can only be taken by the appropriate senior manager, and the employee will be provided in writing with reasons for dismissal, the date on which the employment will terminate, and the right of appeal.

If some sanction short of dismissal is imposed, the employee will receive details of the complaint, will be warned that dismissal could result if there is no satisfactory improvement, and will be advised of the right of appeal. A copy of the written warning will be kept by the supervisor but will be disregarded for disciplinary purposes after ... months subject to achievement and sustainment of satisfactory conduct or performance.

Gross misconduct

The following list provides some examples of offences which are normally regarded as gross misconduct:

- theft or fraud

- physical violence or bullying

- deliberate and serious damage to property

- serious misuse of an organisation's property or name

- deliberately accessing internet sites containing pornographic, offensive or obscene material

- serious insubordination

- unlawful discrimination or harassment

- bringing the organisation into serious disrepute

- serious incapability at work brought on by alcohol or illegal drugs

- causing loss, damage or injury through serious negligence

- a serious breach of health and safety rules

- a serious breach of confidence.

If you are accused of an act of gross misconduct, you may be suspended from work on full pay, normally for no more than five working days, while the alleged offence is investigated. If, on completion of the investigation and the full disciplinary procedure, the organisation is satisfied that gross misconduct has occurred, the result will normally be summary dismissal without notice or payment in lieu of notice.

Appeals

An employee who wishes to appeal against a disciplinary decision must do so within five working days. The senior manager will hear all appeals and his/her decision is final. At the appeal any disciplinary penalty imposed will be reviewed.

Sample disciplinary procedure (small organisation)

1. Purpose and scope

The organisation's aim is to encourage improvement in individual conduct or performance. This procedure sets out the action which will be taken when disciplinary rules are breached.

2. Principles

a) The procedure is designed to establish the facts quickly and to deal consistently with disciplinary issues. No disciplinary action will be taken until the matter has been fully investigated.

5

b) At every stage employees will be informed in writing of what is alleged and have the opportunity to state their case at a disciplinary meeting and be represented or accompanied, if they wish, by a trade union representative or a work colleague.

c) An employee has the right to appeal against any disciplinary penalty.

3. The Procedure

Stage 1 – first warning
If conduct or performance is unsatisfactory, the employee will be given a written warning or performance note. Such warnings will be recorded, but disregarded after ... months of satisfactory service. The employee will also be informed that a final written warning may be considered if there is no sustained satisfactory improvement or change. (Where the first offence is sufficiently serious, for example because it is having, or is likely to have, a serious harmful effect on the organisation, it may be justifiable to move directly to a final written warning.)

Stage 2 – final written warning
If the offence is serious, or there is no improvement in standards, or if a further offence of a similar kind occurs, a final written warning will be given which will include the reason for the warning and a note that if no improvement results within ...

months, action at Stage 3 will be taken.

Stage 3 – dismissal or action short of dismissal
If the conduct or performance has failed to improve, the employee may suffer demotion, disciplinary transfer, loss of seniority (as allowed in the contract) or dismissal.

Gross misconduct
If, after investigation, it is confirmed that an employee has committed an offence of the following nature (the list is not exhaustive), the normal consequence will be dismissal without notice or payment in lieu of notice:

– theft, damage to property, fraud, incapacity for work due to being under the influence of alcohol or illegal drugs, physical violence, bullying and gross insubordination.

While the alleged gross misconduct is being investigated, the employee may be suspended, during which time he or she will be paid their normal pay rate. Any decision to dismiss will be taken by the employer only after full investigation.

Appeals
An employee who wishes to appeal against any disciplinary decision must do so to the named person in the organisation within five working days. The employer will hear the appeal and decide the case as impartially as possible.

Sample grievance procedure (small organisation)

Dealing with grievances informally

If you have a grievance or complaint to do with your work or the people you work with you should, wherever possible, start by talking it over with your manager. You may be able to agree a solution informally between you.

Formal grievance

If the matter is serious and/or you wish to raise the matter formally you should set out the grievance in writing to your manager. You should stick to the facts and avoid language that is insulting or abusive.

Where your grievance is against your manager and you feel unable to approach him or her you should talk to another manager or the owner.

Grievance hearing

Your manager will call you to a meeting, normally within five days, to discuss your grievance. You have the right to be accompanied by a colleague or trade union representative at this meeting if you make a reasonable request.

After the meeting the manager will give you a decision in writing, normally within 24 hours.

Appeal

If you are unhappy with your manager's decision and you wish to appeal you should let your manager know.

You will be invited to an appeal meeting, normally within five days, and your appeal will be heard by a more senior manager (or the company owner). You have the right to be accompanied by a colleague or trade union representative at this meeting if you make a reasonable request.

After the meeting the manager (or owner) will give you a decision, normally within 24 hours. The manager's (or owner's) decision is final.

5

Appendix 3 *sample letters*

Contents

(1) Notice of disciplinary meeting

Date ....

Dear ....

I am writing to tell you that you are required to attend a disciplinary meeting on .... at .... am/pm which is to be held in ....
At this meeting the question of disciplinary action against you, in accordance with the Company Disciplinary Procedure, will be considered with regard to:

I enclose the following documents*:

The possible consequences arising from this meeting might be:

You are entitled, if you wish, to be accompanied by another work colleague or a trade union representative.

Yours sincerely

6

Signed Manager ....

Note:
* Delete if not applicable

(2) Notice of written warning or final written warning

Date ....

Dear ....

You attended a disciplinary hearing on .... I am writing to inform you of your written warning/final written warning*.

This warning will be placed in your personal file but will be disregarded for disciplinary purposes after a period of .... months, provided your conduct improves/performance reaches a satisfactory level**.

a) The nature of the unsatisfactory conduct or performance was:

b) The conduct or performance improvement expected is:

c) The timescale within which the improvement is required is:

d) The likely consequence of further misconduct or insufficient improvement is:

Final written warning/dismissal

You have the right to appeal against this decision (in writing**) to .... within .... days of receiving this disciplinary decision.

Yours sincerely

Signed Manager ....

Note:
* *The wording should be amended as appropriate*
** *Delete as appropriate*

(3) Notice of appeal meeting against warning

Date ....

Dear ....

You have appealed against the written warning/final written warning*
confirmed to you in writing on ....

Your appeal will be heard by .... in .... on ....
at ....

You are entitled to be accompanied by a work colleague or trade union
representative.

The decision of this appeal hearing is final and there is no further right of
review.

Yours sincerely

6

Signed Manager ....

Note:
* *The wording should be amended as appropriate*

(4) Notice of result of appeal against warning

Date ....

Dear ....

You appealed against the decision of the disciplinary hearing that you be given a .... warning/in accordance with the Company Disciplinary Procedure. The appeal hearing was held on ....

I am now writing to inform you of the decision taken by the Manager who conducted the appeal hearing, namely that the decision to .... stands*/the decision to .... be revoked* [specify if no disciplinary action is being taken or what the new disciplinary action is].

You have now exercised your right of appeal under the Company Disciplinary Procedure and this decision is final.

Yours sincerely

Signed Manager ....

Note:
* *The wording should be amended as appropriate*

(5) Letter to be sent by the employer to arrange a meeting where dismissal or action short of dismissal* is being considered

Date ....

Dear ....

I am writing to tell you that .... [insert organisation name] is considering dismissing OR taking disciplinary action [insert proposed action] against you.

This action is being considered with regard to the following circumstances: You are invited to attend a disciplinary meeting on .... at .... am/pm which is to be held in .... where this will be discussed.

You are entitled, if you wish, to be accompanied by another work colleague or your trade union representative.

Yours sincerely

Signed Manager ....

Note:
* Action other than a warning such as transfer or demotion (see p30)

6

(6) Letter to be sent by the employer after the disciplinary meeting arranged in Letter 5

Date ....

Dear ....

On .... you were informed that .... [insert organisation name] was considering dismissing OR taking disciplinary action [insert proposed action] against you.

This was discussed in a meeting on .... At this meeting, it was decided that: [delete as applicable]

Your conduct/performance/etc was still unsatisfactory and that you be dismissed.

Your conduct/performance/etc was still unsatisfactory and that the following disciplinary action would be taken against you ....

No further action would be taken against you.

I am therefore writing to you to confirm the decision that you be dismissed and that your last day of service with the Company will be ....

The reasons for your dismissal are:
I am therefore writing to you to confirm the decision that disciplinary action will be taken against you. The action will be .... The reasons for this disciplinary action are:

You have the right of appeal against this decision. Please [write] to .... within .... days of receiving this disciplinary decision

Yours sincerely

Signed Manager ....

(7) Notice of appeal meeting against dismissal/disciplinary action*

Date ....

Dear ....

You have appealed against your dismissal/disciplinary action [delete as appropriate] on .... confirmed to you in writing on ....
Your appeal will be heard by .... in .... on ....
at ....

You are entitled, if you wish, to be accompanied by another work colleague or a trade union representative.

The decision of this appeal meeting is final and there is no further right of review.

Yours sincerely

6

Signed Manager ....

Note:
* *Action other than a warning such as transfer or demotion* (see p30)

(8) Notice of result of appeal against dismissal/disciplinary action*

Date ....

Dear ....

You appealed against the decision of the disciplinary hearing that you be dismissed/subject to disciplinary action [delete as appropriate].

The appeal meeting was held on ....

I am now writing to inform you of the decision taken by ....

[insert name of the manager] who conducted the appeal meeting, namely that the decision to .... stands/ the decision to .... be revoked [specify if no disciplinary action is being taken or what the new disciplinary action is].

You have now exercised your right of appeal under the Company Disciplinary Procedure and this decision is final.

Yours sincerely

Signed Manager ....

Note:
* *Action other than a warning such as transfer or demotion (see p30)*

(9) Letter of enquiry regarding likely cause of absence addressed to a worker's general practitioner

Date ....

Doctor's name ....

Address ....

....

PLEASE ACKNOWLEDGE RECEIPT OF THIS LETTER IF THERE IS LIKELY TO BE ANY DELAY IN REPLYING

Re ....

Name ....

Address ....

....

To administer Statutory Sick Pay, and the Company's sick pay scheme, and to plan the work in the department, it would be helpful to have a report on your patient, who works for our organisation.

His/her work as a .... has the following major features:

Management responsibility for
Seated/standing/mobile
Light/medium/heavy effort required
Day/shift/night work
Clerical/secretarial duties
Group I (private)/Group II (professional) driver
Other

The absence record for the past year is summarised as:

Total days lost
This month
Previous months

Attached is your patient's permission to enquire. He/she wishes/does not wish to have access to the report under the Access to Medical Reports Act 1988:

What is the likely date of return to work?

Will there be any disability at that time?

How long is it likely to last?

Are there any reasonable adjustments we could make to accommodate the disability?

Is there any underlying medical reason for this attendance record?

Is he/she likely to be able to render regular and efficient service in the future?

Is there any specific recommendation you wish to make about him/her which would help in finding him/her an alternative job, if that is necessary, and if there is an opportunity for redeployment (for instance no climbing ladders, no driving).

I would be grateful for an early reply and enclose a stamped addressed envelope. Please attach your account to the report (following the BMA guidance on fees).

Yours sincerely

Signed Name (BLOCK LETTERS) ....

Role in the company ....

Note:
Please amend/delete where necessary

Appendix 4 Dealing with absence

This appendix considers how to handle problems of absence and gives guidance about unauthorised short-term and long-term absences, and the failure to return from extended leave. More extensive advice on attendance management is available in the Acas advisory booklet Managing attendance and employee turnover available to purchase or download on the Acas website www.acas.org.uk. A distinction should be made between absence on grounds of illness or injury and absence for no good reason which may call for disciplinary action. Where disciplinary action is called for, the normal disciplinary procedure should be used. Where the employee is absent because of illness or injury, the guidance in this section of the booklet should be followed. The organisation should be aware of the requirements of the Equality Act 2010 when making any decisions that affect someone who may be disabled as defined by the Act[12].

Records showing lateness and the duration of and reasons for all spells of absence should be kept to help monitor absence levels. These enable management to check levels of absence or lateness so that problems can be spotted and addressed at an early stage (the Information Commissioner[13] has produced a Code of Practice on employment records).

How should frequent and persistent short-term absence be handled?

- unexpected absences should be investigated promptly and the employee asked for an explanation at a return-to-work interview

- if there are no acceptable reasons then the employer may wish to treat the matter as a conduct issue and deal with it under the disciplinary procedure

- where there is no medical certificate to support frequent short-term, self-certified, absences then the employee should be asked to see a doctor to establish whether treatment is necessary and whether the underlying reason for the absence is work-related. If no medical support is forthcoming the employer should consider whether to take action under the disciplinary procedure

- if the absence could be disability related the employer should consider what reasonable adjustments could be made in the workplace to help the employee (this might be something as simple as an adequate, ergonomic chair, or a power-assisted piece of equipment[14]. Reasonable adjustment also means redeployment to a different type of work if necessary

- if the absence is because of temporary problems relating to dependants, the employee may be entitled to have time off under the provisions of the Employment Rights Act 1996 relating to time off for dependants

- if the absence is because the employee has difficulty managing both work and home responsibilities then the employer should give serious consideration to more flexible ways of working. Employees have the right to request flexible working arrangements – including job-sharing, part-time working, flexi-time, working from home/teleworking and school time contracts – and employers must have a good business reason for rejecting any application

- in all cases the employee should be told what improvement in attendance is expected and warned of the likely consequences if this does not happen

- if there is no improvement, the employee's length of service, performance, the likelihood of a change in attendance, the availability of suitable alternative work where appropriate, and the effect of past and future absences on the organisation should all be taken into account in deciding appropriate action.

In order to show both the employee concerned, and other employees, that absence is regarded as a serious matter and may result in dismissal, it is very important that persistent absence is dealt with promptly, firmly and consistently.

An examination of records will identify those employees who are frequently absent and may show an absence pattern.

How should longer-term absence through ill health be handled?

Where absence is due to medically certificated illness, the issue becomes one of capability rather than conduct. Employers need to take a more sympathetic and considerate approach, particularly if the employee is disabled and where reasonable adjustments at the workplace might enable them to return to work.

There are certain steps an employer should take when considering the problem of long-term absence:

- employee and employer should keep in regular contact with each other

- the employee must be kept fully informed if there is any risk to employment

- if the employer wishes to contact the employee's doctor, he or she must notify the employee in writing that they intend to make such an application and they must secure the employee's consent in writing[15]. The employer must inform the individual that he or she has:

  - the right to withhold consent to the application being made

  - the right to state that he or she wishes to have access to the report. (The Access to Medical Reports Act 1988 also gives the individual the right to have access to the medical practitioner's report for up to six months after it was supplied)

  - rights concerning access to the report before (and/or after) it is supplied

  - the right to withhold consent to the report being supplied to the employer

- the right to request amendments to the report

- where the employee states that he or she wishes to have access to the report, the employer must let the GP know this when making the application and at the same time let the employee know that the report has been requested

- the letter of enquiry reproduced in Appendix 3 – Sample letters, and approved by the British Medical Association, may be used, and the employee's permission to the enquiry should be attached to the letter[16]

- the employee must contact the GP within 21 days of the date of application to make arrangement to see the report. Otherwise the rights under the 1988 Act will be lost

- if the employee considers the report to be incorrect or misleading, the employee may make a written request to the GP to make appropriate amendments

- if the GP refuses, the employee has the right to ask the GP to attach a statement to the report reflecting the employee's view on any matters of disagreement

- the employee may withhold consent to the report being supplied to the employer

- on the basis of the GP's report the employer should consider whether alternative work is available

- the employer is not expected to create a special job for the employee concerned, nor to be a medical expert, but to take action on the basis of the medical evidence

- where there is a reasonable doubt about the nature of the illness or injury, the employee should be asked if he or she would agree to be examined by a doctor to be appointed by the organisation

- where an employee refuses to cooperate in providing medical evidence, or to undergo an independent medical examination, the employee should be told in writing that a decision will be taken on the basis of the information available and that it could result in dismissal

- where the employee is allergic to a product used in the workplace the employer should consider remedial action or a transfer to alternative work

- where the employee's job can no longer be held open, and no suitable alternative work is available, the employee should be informed of the likelihood of dismissal

- where dismissal action is taken the employee should be given the period of notice to which he or she is entitled by statute or contract and informed of any right of appeal.

Where an employee has been on long-term sick absence and there is little likelihood of he or she becoming fit enough to return, it may be argued that the contract of employment has been terminated through 'frustration'. However, the doctrine of frustration should not be relied on since the courts are generally reluctant to apply it where a procedure exists for termination of the contract. It is therefore better for the employer to take dismissal action after following proper procedures.

Specific health problems
Consideration should be given to introducing measures to help employees, regardless of status or seniority, who are suffering from alcohol or drug abuse, or from stress. The aim should be to identify employees affected and encourage them to seek help and treatment. See the Acas advisory booklet Health, work and wellbeing available

to purchase or download on the Acas website www.acas.org.uk Employers should consider whether it is appropriate to treat the problem as a medical rather than a disciplinary matter.

There is sometimes workforce pressure to dismiss an employee because of a medical condition, or even threats of industrial action. If such an employee is dismissed, then he or she may be able to claim unfair dismissal before an employment tribunal, or breach of contract. Also, the Equality Act 2010 makes it unlawful for an employer of any size to treat a disabled person less favourably for a reason relating to their disability, without a justifiable reason. Employers are required to make a reasonable adjustment to working conditions or the workplace where that would help to accommodate a particular disabled person[17].

Failure to return from extended leave on the agreed date

Employers may have policies which allow employees extended leave of absence without pay, for example to visit relatives in their countries of origin, or relatives who have emigrated to other countries, or to nurse a sick relative. There is no general statutory right to such leave without pay, except to deal with an initial emergency relating to a dependant under the Employment Rights Act 1996.

Where a policy of extended leave is in operation, the following points should be borne in mind:

● the policy should apply to all employees, irrespective of their age, sex, marital or civil partnership status, pregnancy and maternity, racial group, disability, sexual orientation, gender reassignment, or religion or belief

● any conditions attaching to the granting of extended leave should be carefully explained to the employee, using interpreters if necessary, and the employee's signature should be obtained as an acknowledgement that he or she understands and accepts them. Employers should be aware that agreed extended leave can preserve continuity of employment, even when such leave is unpaid and other terms and conditions of employment are suspended for the duration of the leave

● if an employee fails to return on the agreed date, this should be approached in the same way as any other failure to abide by the rules and the circumstances should be investigated in the normal way, with disciplinary procedures being followed if appropriate

7

- care should be taken to ensure that foreign medical certificates are not treated in a discriminatory way: employees can fall ill while abroad just as they can fall ill in this country

- before deciding to dismiss an employee who overstays leave, the employee's experience, length of service, reliability record and any explanation given should all be taken into account

- failure to return from ordinary maternity leave does not of itself terminate the contract of employment. Employers should try and find out the reason for the failure and take action if necessary as in any other case of failing to return from leave (whether extended/additional maternity/holiday/parental/time off for dependants).

An agreement that an employee should return to work on a particular date will not prevent a complaint of unfair dismissal to an employment tribunal if the employee is dismissed for failing to return as agreed. In all such cases, all the factors mentioned above and the need to act reasonably should be borne in mind before any dismissal action is taken.

Appendix 5 Basic principles of the Data Protection Act 1998 and The Equality Act 2010

Data Protection Act 1998

The Data Protection Act gives individuals the right to know what information is held about them. It provides a framework to ensure that personal information is handled properly.

The Act works in two ways. Firstly, it states that anyone who processes personal information must comply with eight principles, which make sure that personal information is:

- fairly and lawfully processed

- processed for limited purposes

- adequate, relevant and not excessive

- accurate and up to date

- not kept for longer than is necessary

- processed in line with your rights

- secure

- not transferred to other countries without adequate protection.

The second area covered by the Act provides individuals with important rights, including the right to find out what personal information is held on computer and most paper records.

Should an individual or organisation feel they're being denied access to personal information they're entitled to, or feel their information has not been handled according to the eight principles, they can contact the Information Commissioner's Office for help. Complaints are usually dealt with informally, but if this isn't possible, enforcement action can be taken.

Full details are available from the Information Commissioner's Office, Wycliffe House, Water Lane, Wilmslow, Cheshire SK9 5AF, Information line **01625 545700**. The website, www.ico.org.uk provides comprehensive advice including details of the Code of Practice on the Use of Personal Data in Employer/ Employee Relationships and other Codes of Practice on recruitment and selection, employment records, monitoring at work and medical information.

7

8

The Equality Act 2010

The Equality Act gives disabled people rights in employment. A disabled person is defined in the Act as 'anyone with a physical or mental impairment which has a substantial and long-term adverse effect upon his or her ability to carry out normal day-to-day activities'.

However, disability does not necessarily affect someone's health, so insisting on a medical report purely on the basis of the disability may be unlawful discrimination. If your organisation believes that pre- employment health screening is necessary, you must make sure it is carried out in a non-discriminatory way. It is unlawful to ask health related questions before making a job offer (whether condition or unconditional), except in order to:

● determine if a candidate can carry out a function which is essential to the job

● ask whether candidates need special arrangements for any part of the application process

● anonymously monitor whether candidates are disabled

● take positive action to assist disabled people

● check that a candidate has a disability where this is a genuine requirement of the job.

If a report from any individual's doctor is sought, then permission must be given by the individual, and they have the right to see the report (Access to Medical Reports Act 1988).

Discrimination means treating someone less favourably without any justification, and the Act requires that employers make reasonable adjustments if that will then remove the reason for the unfavourable treatment. An example of a reasonable adjustment could be the provision of a suitable computer keyboard to an operator who had difficulty through disability in using a conventional keyboard.

In relation to discipline and grievance procedures, employers must clearly ensure they do not discriminate in any area of practice which could lead to dismissal or any other detriment (for example warnings).

The Act also covers people who become disabled during the course of their employment, and this is particularly relevant to the absence handling section of this handbook. It is vital that the employer should discuss with the worker what their needs really are and what effect, if any, the disability may have on future work with the organisation. Any dismissal of a disabled employee for a reason relating to the disability would have to be justified, and the reason for it would have to be one which could not be removed or made less than substantial by any reasonable adjustment.

The Equality and Human Rights Commission provides information and advice about all aspects of the Equality Act 2010, as well as signposting specialist organisations where necessary. In addition, it can offer good practice advice on the employment of disabled people. Tel: England **0845 604 6610**, Scotland **0845 604 5510** and for Wales **0845 604 8810**.

8

Appendix 6 *Important changes to making Employment Tribunal claims*

Previously, an employee could go straight to the tribunal service, but this will change. From 6 April 2014, if an employee is considering making an Employment Tribunal claim against their employer, they should notify Acas that they intend to submit a claim.

Details of how and where to do this are given below.

Acas will, in most circumstances, offer to assist in settling differences between employee and employer. Employers intending to make a counter-claim against an employee must follow a similar procedure.

The process for agreeing settlement is called Early Conciliation. It is handled by experienced Acas conciliators and support officers and is:

- free of charge

- impartial and non-judgmental

- confidential

- independent of the Employment Tribunal service

- offered in addition to existing conciliation services.

Early Conciliation focuses on resolving matters on terms that employee and employer agree.

Early Conciliation may not resolve matters in every claim. When this is the case Acas will issue a certificate that is now required for a claim to be submitted to an Employment Tribunal.

From July 2013, employees have been required to pay a fee to "lodge" a claim at the Employment Tribunal, followed by another fee if the claim progresses to a tribunal hearing. In some cases, other fees may also apply. If a claim is successful, the employee may apply for the costs of the fees to be covered by the employer. Some employees, including those on low incomes, may be exempt from fees.

Remember, when a claim is lodged with a tribunal, Acas will continue to offer conciliation to both sides until the tribunal makes a judgment and, if the claim is successful, a remedy decision (usually financial compensation) has been made.

To find out more about
Early Conciliation, go to
www.acas.org.uk/earlyconciliation

To find out more about
Employment Tribunal fees, go to
www.justice.gov.uk/tribunals/
employment

9

Glossary

capability: an employee's ability or qualification to do their job. Most often referred to in discipline cases where there is a lack of capability

conduct: an employee's behaviour in the workplace

disciplinary action: formal action against an employee: for example issuing a first written warning for misconduct or dismissing someone for gross misconduct

disciplinary procedure: is a procedure for organisations to follow to deal with cases of misconduct or unsatisfactory performance. It helps employers deal with discipline cases fairly and consistently

employees: are people who work for an employer under a contract of employment. The term is used throughout Sections 1 & 2 of the handbook and the Code of Practice

grievance: is a problem or concern that an employee has about their work, working conditions or relationships with colleagues

grievance procedure: is a procedure for organisations to use to consider employees' grievances. It helps employers deal with grievances fairly and consistently

gross misconduct: are acts which are so serious as to justify possible dismissal see example list on p31

improvement note: in cases of unsatisfactory performance an employee should be given an improvement note setting out the performance problem, the improvement that is required, the timescale for achieving this improvement, a review date and any support the employer will provide to assist the employee

natural justice: refers to the basic fundamental principles of fair treatment. These principles include the duty to give someone a fair hearing; the duty to ensure that the matter is decided by someone who is impartial; and the duty to allow an appeal against a decision

reasonable adjustments: a way of preventing discrimination against disabled employees by making changes to ensure that they are not at a disadvantage. For example, a specialist keyboard would count as a reasonable adjustment for a disabled employee unable to use a conventional keyboard

sanction: is a punishment imposed on an employee as a result of unsatisfactory performance or misconduct. Sanctions may include dismissal or actions short of dismissal such as loss of pay or demotion

summary dismissal: is dismissal without notice – usually only justifiable for gross misconduct. Summary is not necessarily the same as instant and incidents of gross misconduct should be investigated as part of a formal procedure

workers: is a term that includes employees and also other groups such as agency workers or anyone carrying out work who is not genuinely self-employed. Workers might include those involved in seasonal work – such as farm labourers or shop assistants.

10

Acas Training

Our training is carried out by experienced Acas staff who work with businesses every day. They will show you the value to your business of following best practice in employment matters and how to avoid the common pitfalls. We also run special training sessions on new legislation.

Look at the Acas website for up-to-date information about all our training or if you want to book a place online, just go to www.acas.org.uk/training or call the Acas customer services team on 0300 123 1150.

Training sessions are specially designed for smaller companies and our current programme includes:

- Managing discipline and grievances at work

- Managing absence at work

- Employment law update

- HR management for beginners

- Having difficult conversations

- Contracts of employment: how to get it right

- New employment legislation

- Redundancy and restructuring.

We also have free online learning to help you – just go to www.acas.org.uk and click on e-learning to look at the topics covered.

Acas Publications

Book time with your Employment specialist

Whether you need to know how to write a contract of employment, how much holiday you are entitled to or about the latest employment legislation, our range of publications give practical information and advice for both employers and employees on employment matters.

View and order online at www.acas.org.uk/publications.

You can also sign up for Acas' free e-newsletter. It will keep you informed about the latest developments in employment legislation as well as best practice advice on a range of employment-related topics.

If you would like to join our mailing list, subscribe online at www.acas.org.uk/subscribe.

Notes

1. For detailed advice on absence see the Acas Advisory Booklet Managing attendance and employee turnover.

2. Further advice and Codes of Practice may be obtained from the Equality and Human Rights Commission at **www.equalityhumanrights.com**.

3. See the Acas Guidance on Age and the workplace: putting the Equality Act 2010 and the removal of the default retirement age (DRA) 2011 into practice.

4. Guidance on what the written statement must include is provided on **www.gov.uk**.

5. The recommendations for good practice can be obtained from the Information Commissioner's Office, Wycliffe House, Water Lane, Wilmslow, Cheshire SK9 5AF Tel 01625 545700 **www.ico.org.uk**.

6. Guidance given by the Employment Appeal Tribunal in Linfood Cash and Carry v Thomson [1989] IRLR 235, sets out the approach that should be taken with anonymous informants. In particular statements should be in writing, available to the accused employee and give details of time/place/dates as appropriate. The employer should enquire as to the character of the informant and assess the credibility and weight to be attached to the evidence.

7. Special consideration should be given before imposing disciplinary suspension without pay. It must be allowed for in the worker's contract of employment, and no suspension should exceed the maximum period set out in the contract. It must not be unreasonably prolonged, since it would then be open to the worker to take action for breach of contract or resign and claim constructive dismissal.

8. Section 92 of the Employment Rights Act 1996 refers. More details of employees' Rights to notice and reasons for dismissal is provided on **www.gov.uk**.

9. In law, frustration occurs when, without the fault of either party, some event, which was not reasonably foreseeable at the time of the contract, renders future performance either impossible or something radically different from what was contemplated originally. Legal advice should be sought if it is thought frustration of the employment contract has occurred.

10. The recommendations for good practice can be obtained from the Information Commissioner's Office, Wycliffe House, Water Lane, Wilmslow, Cheshire SK9 5AF Tel **01625 545700** **www.ico.org.uk**.

11. See advice leaflet – Bullying and harassment at work: a guide for managers and employers.

12. For further information see the Equality and Human Rights Commission website at **www.equalityhumanrights.com**.

13. See the Information Commissioner's website at **www.ico.org.uk**.

14. For further information see the Equality and Human Rights Commission website at **www.equalityhumanrights.com**.

15. Access to Medical Reports Act 1988

16. The GP should return the report via the company doctor. If there is not one the employer should make it clear to the employee, when seeking permission to approach the GP, that the report will be sent direct to the employer. Employers who wish to seek advice on securing the services of a company doctor should contact the Faculty of Occupational Medicine at 6 St Andrews Place, Regents Park, London NW1 4LB Tel **020 7317 589010** **www.facoccmed.ac.uk**.

17. For further information see the Equality and human rights commission website at **www.equalityhumanrights.com**.

part of Williams Lea

Published by TSO (The Stationery Office) and available from:

Online
www.tsoshop.co.uk

Mail, Telephone, Fax & E-mail
TSO
PO Box 29, Norwich, NR3 1GN
Telephone orders/General enquiries: 0870 600 5522
Fax orders: 0870 600 5533
E-mail: customer.services@tso.co.uk
Textphone 0870 240 3701

TSO@Blackwell and other Accredited Agents

First published 2015

ISBN 9780117082816